SEA HUNTERS

SEA HUNTERS

Lionel Bender and Alwyne Wheeler

CHANCELLOR
PRESS

First published in Great Britain by Franklin Watts
in 3 separate volumes under the titles:

Sharks 1987
Whales and Dolphins 1988
Crocodiles and Alligators 1987

© Aladdin Books Limited
28 Percy Street
London W1P 9FF

This omnibus edition first published in 1993 by
Chancellor Press, an imprint of Reed Consumer Books Limited
Michelin House, 81 Fulham Road, London SW3 6RB
and Auckland, Melbourne, Singapore and Toronto

A CIP catalogue record for this book is available at
the British Library

ISBN 1 85152 290 5

Printed in Hong Kong

CONTENTS

Design
David West
Children's Book Design
Illustrations
Louise Nevett
Tessa Barwick
Picture Research
Cecilia Weston-Baker
Editor
Kate Petty

This book tells you about sharks – how they live, what they look like and how they survive in the ocean today. Find out some surprising facts in the boxes on each page. The Identification Chart at the back will help you when you see sharks in zoos or aquaria.

or

The little square shows you the size of the shark. Each side represents about three metres.

A red square means that a shark is being studied by scientists. Turn to the Survival File.

The picture opposite is a White-tip Shark photographed in the Red Sea

SHARKS

Alwyne Wheeler

Introduction

There were plenty of sharks in the sea 350 million years ago, long before mammals, birds or other fishes were common. So sharks are survivors of the prehistoric age, ideally suited to the world they live in. There are about 340 different kinds of shark known today. Many of them are magnificent creatures.

Like all other animals, sharks need to be protected – perhaps more so, because so few people like them. In fact, most sharks live far out to sea and are unlikely to attack a human.

Scientists are trying to find out more about sharks. Bathers might be able to avoid attack if they understand why sharks behave in a certain way.

Streamlined for speed

Sharks are perfectly built for life in the sea. Their streamlined shape and the way in which the high tail fin is balanced by the pectoral fins means that they can swim and dive effortlessly. Their long tails drive them along at a gentle cruising speed. When hunting they can travel at about 35 kph to catch fast-swimming animals such as squids, anchovies and flying fishes.

Many sharks, like the Blue Shark, are powerful long-distance swimmers too. Blue Sharks are found all round the world where the sea is warm. In summertime they follow the warmer water. Blue Sharks live near the surface. The clear blue of their backs and pure white colouring of the underside are typical of sharks which live near the surface of the sea.

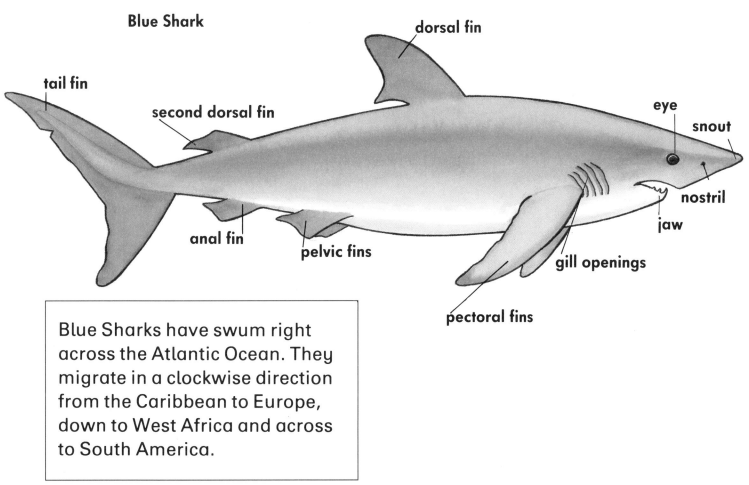

Blue Shark

dorsal fin

tail fin

second dorsal fin

eye

snout

anal fin

pelvic fins

nostril

jaw

gill openings

pectoral fins

Blue Sharks have swum right across the Atlantic Ocean. They migrate in a clockwise direction from the Caribbean to Europe, down to West Africa and across to South America.

◁ **A Blue Shark, perfect swimming machine**

Non-stop swimmers

Active sharks which live near the surface of the sea, like the White-tip Shark, keep moving all their lives. They never stop swimming and go to sleep. Sharks that live on the seabed may lie still for hours on end. Some may find underwater caves in which they can snooze. Unlike most fishes, sharks do not have an air bladder to help them float. Instead they have a large oily liver which does the same job.

Sharks get a constant supply of oxygen when they swim continuously. A steady stream of water flows over their gills and out of the five gill slits on each side of the head. The gills extract oxygen from the water. If the shark stops swimming or is trapped, the water no longer flows over its gills. Then it cannot take in oxygen and it drowns.

White-tip Shark

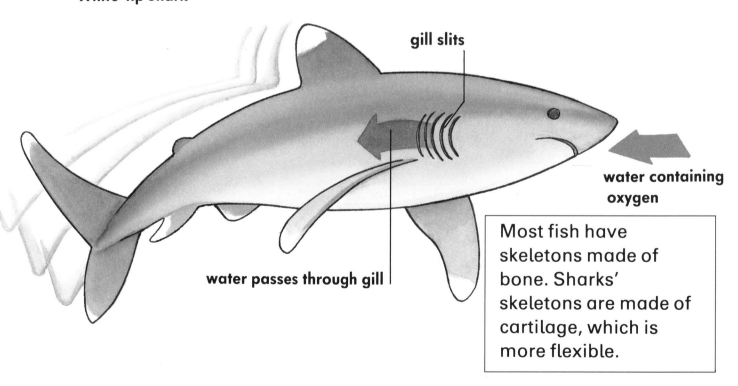

gill slits

water containing oxygen

water passes through gill

Most fish have skeletons made of bone. Sharks' skeletons are made of cartilage, which is more flexible.

The White-tip Shark is probably the most common of the big sharks in the open sea ▷

Extra senses

Sharks depend very heavily on smell to find their food.
Their nostrils are quite large and far apart. When
searching for food sharks swing their heads from side
to side and turn to where they smell the strongest
scent. Scientists think that sharks sometimes bump
an object to "taste" it through taste cells in the skin.
Incredibly sensitive cells on a shark's snout pick up the
tiniest electrical discharges from a nearby animal.
They can also feel vibrations along the sensitive
"lateral line" when an animal is struggling in the
water. On top of all this, they can smell blood in the
water even when it is diluted ten million times. So they
do not depend on their eyesight to hunt their prey.

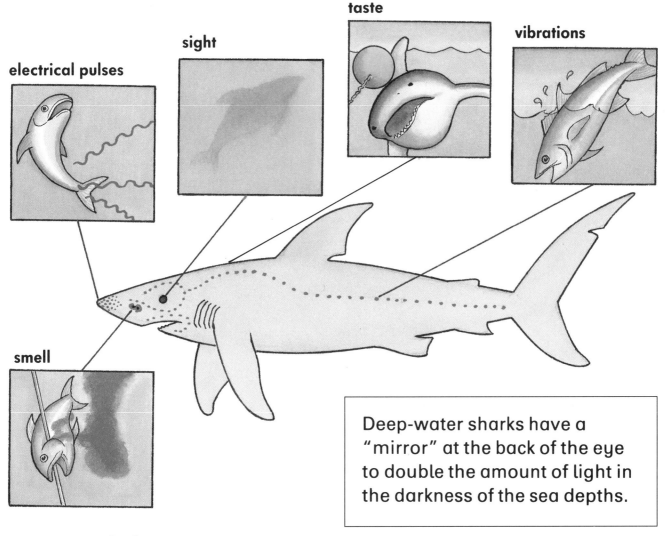

taste

sight

vibrations

electrical pulses

smell

Deep-water sharks have a
"mirror" at the back of the eye
to double the amount of light in
the darkness of the sea depths.

◁ **A Lemon Shark**

Teeth for biting

Sharks never stop growing new teeth. All of them have many rows of teeth in both jaws. As the front ones wear down and fall out they are replaced by new teeth from inside the jaw. The Lemon Shark replaces about 30 teeth each week.

The shape of a shark's teeth depends on the food it eats. The Tiger Shark often eats turtles. It has saw-edged teeth in both jaws. It bites the turtle and then shakes its head slowly from side to side so that the teeth saw through the shell and bones. The Port Jackson Shark has large, flat teeth for crushing sea-urchins, prawns and crabs. The Nurse Shark uses its heavy jaws for crushing shellfish while its hundreds of small, pointed teeth hold the food still.

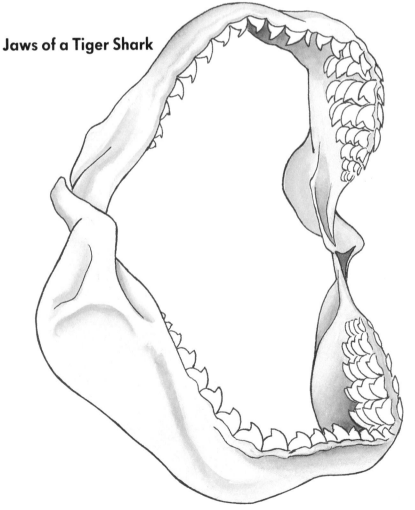

Jaws of a Tiger Shark

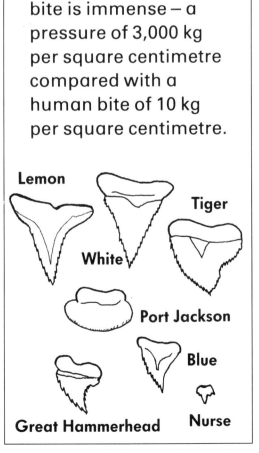

The power of a shark's bite is immense – a pressure of 3,000 kg per square centimetre compared with a human bite of 10 kg per square centimetre.

Lemon

Tiger

White

Port Jackson

Blue

Nurse

Great Hammerhead

A Sand Tiger Shark showing its teeth ▷

Unfussy diet

Most active sharks have sharp-edged or spiky teeth.
They feed on many different kinds of prey. Some, like
the Blue Shark, eat fast-swimming squids and all
kinds of fishes which live in the surface waters. Other
sharks, like the Tiger Shark, seem to eat almost
anything they come across – dolphins, sea mammals,
seabirds and turtles. Fishermen have found old boots,
tin cans, beef bones, floats from fishing nets, the head
of a sheep and even a dead dog inside Tiger Sharks.
Much of this was rubbish dumped in the sea. It is easy
to see why the Tiger Shark has been called the dustbin
of the sea!

When several sharks pick up the scent of blood they
rush in to bite at the prey in a "feeding frenzy".

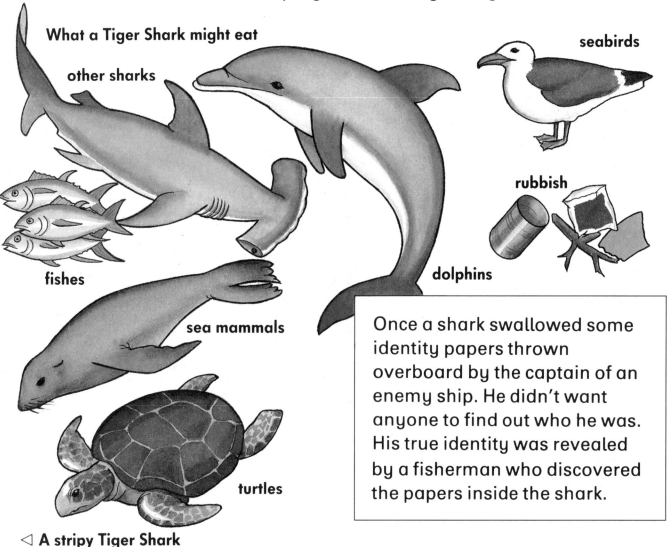

What a Tiger Shark might eat

other sharks

seabirds

fishes

rubbish

dolphins

sea mammals

turtles

Once a shark swallowed some
identity papers thrown
overboard by the captain of an
enemy ship. He didn't want
anyone to find out who he was.
His true identity was revealed
by a fisherman who discovered
the papers inside the shark.

◁ **A stripy Tiger Shark**

Fellow travellers

Sometimes sharks travel in groups but often they hunt alone. Even those lone hunters are usually accompanied by smaller fishes which swim close by. Pilot fishes have dark stripes across their bodies. They hide in the shadow of the shark, protected from their enemies but able to dart out and snap up any suitable food.

Shark suckers and remoras are sucker fish which actually hitch a ride on the shark. They cling to its rough skin by a sucker on top of the head and back. They usually stay close to the shark, feeding on any parasites that attach themselves to it. They also feed on small creatures passing by.

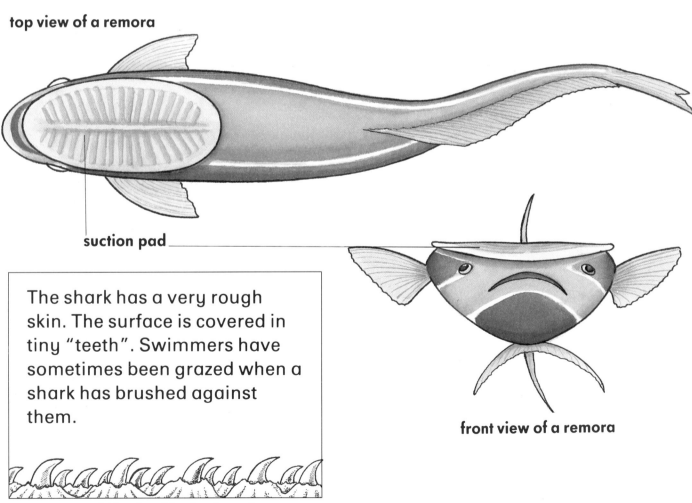

top view of a remora

suction pad

The shark has a very rough skin. The surface is covered in tiny "teeth". Swimmers have sometimes been grazed when a shark has brushed against them.

front view of a remora

◁ **A Leopard Shark with shark suckers**

Gentle giants

Three kinds of very large shark are harmless, slow-moving giants. The Whale Shark, the biggest known shark at 13.7 metres long, lives in tropical seas. It swims along sucking in minute animal plankton. Sometimes it feeds on anchovies, sardines and other small fishes.

Basking Sharks live in cooler, temperate seas and grow up to about 10 metres. They feed on animal plankton by swimming along with their mouths open.

Megamouth has only been found twice. It grows to 4.5 metres. It lives in deep water and feeds only on deep-sea shrimps. They are attracted by light organs that glow inside its huge mouth.

▽ **A Basking Shark with its mouth open**

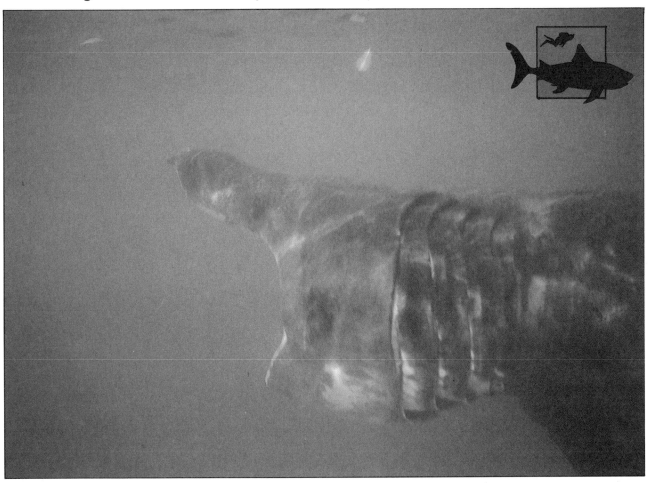

◁ **A Whale Shark**

Unsafe waters

Sometimes swimmers are killed by sharks. Altogether there are around 100 shark attacks on people each year, but only about 25 to 30 of the victims actually die. Almost all attacks take place in the warm waters around the coasts of Australia, South Africa and the warmer coasts of North America. This is partly because the heat seems to make the sharks more aggressive.

Only about 20 kinds of sharks are dangerous. The most dangerous of all is probably the Great White Shark. It grows to at least 6.4 metres, large enough to eat seals, sealions, porpoises and big fishes as well as occasional swimmers. Most sharks attack when they are frightened or threatened by a swimmer's approach rather than because they are hungry.

Sharks are attracted by splashing and struggling. If a shark is near by, a swimmer should swim away strongly and steadily and try not to panic.

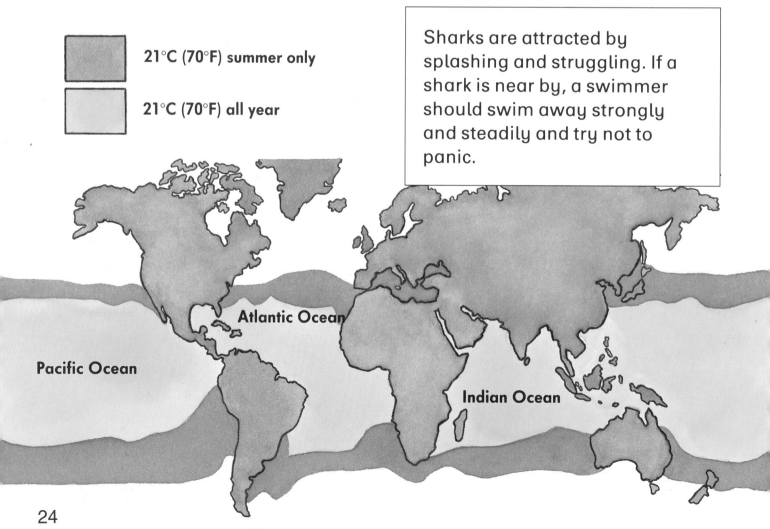

21°C (70°F) summer only

21°C (70°F) all year

Pacific Ocean

Atlantic Ocean

Indian Ocean

Strange sharks

Hammerhead Sharks have flat heads which extend sideways to form a hammer shape. They have an enormous advantage over other sharks. The eyes at the extreme ends of the hammer are able to see all round the shark and their widely-spaced nostrils help them smell food at a great distance. Hammerheads are usually the first sharks to arrive at a bait.

The Wobbegong lives on the coasts of northern Australia and Papua New Guinea, usually close to coral reefs. Its mottled colouring and long fringed beard around its head help it to hide amongst seaweeds and coral. It lies in wait for fishes, crabs, lobsters or octopuses to come close enough to catch.

▽ **A Wobbegong Shark lying near the seabed**

◁ **The strange Hammerhead Shark**

Shark babies

Most fishes lay their eggs in the water, but sharks do not just abandon their eggs. Many shark babies are kept inside the mother's body until they are big enough to swim and feed on their own. The Blue Shark sometimes has as many as 50 babies at a time, but others, like the Porbeagle, have only one or two. A Spurdog carries her 20 babies inside her for nearly two years before they are born.

The Dogfish – a small shark – lays its eggs in small leathery cases. They have long threads at the corners to tangle in seaweed and stop them being washed away. The baby Dogfish hatches out after many months when it is about 10 centimetres in length.

A Dogfish egg is often called a "mermaid's purse"

Dogfish

Shark babies can look after themselves as soon as they are born. They don't stay close to the mother. She takes no further interest in them.

A young Port Jackson Shark ▷

Sharks' enemies

Because many sharks are large and can swim quickly there are very few animals which attack them. Some small or newborn sharks are eaten by bigger sharks, and some are attacked by Orca Whales, Sperm Whales and large fishes. A number of dolphins will attack a shark together to protect their own young. Swordfish have also been known to stab at sharks.

The biggest enemy of sharks is man. About 30 people a year are killed by sharks, but about 4.5 million sharks are killed by people. In some countries sharks like the Dogfish and the Spurdog are used for food.

Dolphins sometimes attack sharks

Shark meat is eaten all over the world. Small sharks sold in fish shops are usually called "flake" or "rock-eel".

Survival file

Sharks have survived for millions of years. But even though their ocean habitat is not in any particular danger, they are at risk from the activities of humans who see them as an evil menace. Luckily, there are scientists who want to study sharks and find out more about them. The best place to watch sharks is in their natural surroundings. Divers sometimes stay inside a cage so they cannot be attacked. Then they can film the sharks at close quarters in safety. They attract the sharks with a bait of fresh fish.

Filming a Great White Shark from a cage

Experienced divers sometimes swim freely among the sharks. They carry a stick with an explosive head on it to stave off the dangerous sharks. They try to understand the sharks' "body language". The way a shark moves when it is swimming towards a diver may tell us whether it is aggressive, frightened, curious, hungry or even playful. Divers "tag" sharks by fastening a number on to a fin. If one is recaptured they can see how it has grown and how far it has travelled.

Diver alongside a Whale Shark

Valerie Taylor testing her shark-suit

Scientists can also learn from sharks kept in captivity. They are studying how they hear, how well they can see, and how much they depend on their sense of smell. They want to find out how the organs that detect faint electric discharges from other animals work. It is important to learn about their sense of taste. If scientists can find a substance that sharks do not like, then swimmers and divers will be able to carry it with them in case of attack.

Some naturalists, like the Taylors, find sharks so fascinating that they have made them a lifetime's study.

Identification chart

This chart shows you some of the more common sharks. You can see some of them in the zoo. The sharks are drawn to scale to show their comparative sizes. The sides of each square of the grid represent 30cms.

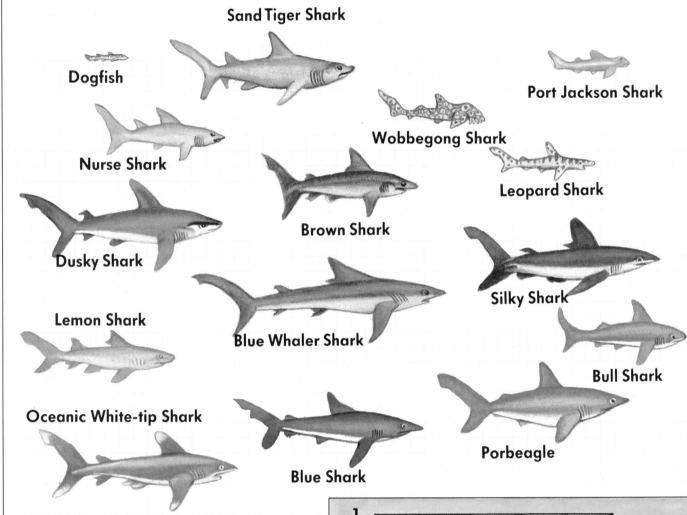

Sand Tiger Shark

Dogfish

Port Jackson Shark

Wobbegong Shark

Nurse Shark

Leopard Shark

Brown Shark

Dusky Shark

Silky Shark

Lemon Shark

Blue Whaler Shark

Bull Shark

Oceanic White-tip Shark

Porbeagle

Blue Shark

Draw a life-size shark

1. Make yourself a huge sheet of paper.
2. Divide it into (roughly) 30-centimetre squares.
3. Copy your shark from these pages, using the squares here to help you.
4. Colour in your shark.
5. Cut it out carefully.
6. You can mount it on stiff card.

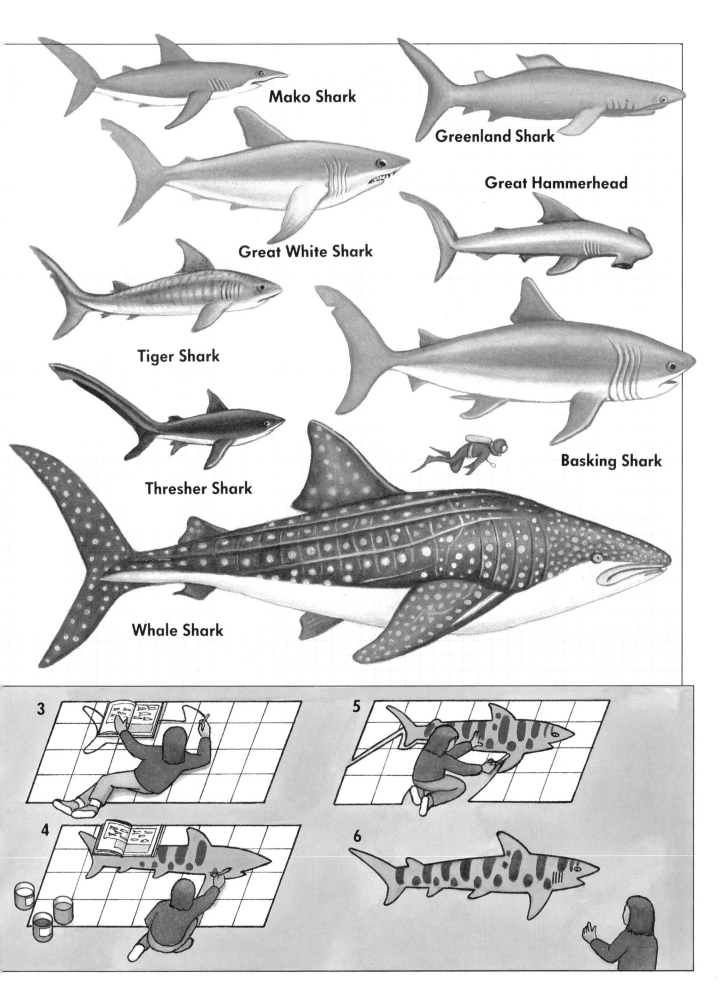

Mako Shark

Greenland Shark

Great Hammerhead

Great White Shark

Tiger Shark

Basking Shark

Thresher Shark

Whale Shark

3

5

4

6

Design
David West
Children's Book Design
Illustrations
George Thompson
Picture Research
Cecilia Weston-Baker
Editor
Denny Robson
Consultant
John Stidworthy

This book is about all the different types of whales – the baleen whales and the toothed whales, including porpoises and dolphins. The Identification Chart at the back of the book will show you their shapes and sizes and indicate the seas and oceans in which they live.

The little square shows you the size of the whale. Each side represents about ten metres.

A red square means that the whale is an endangered species. See the Survival File.

A Humpback Whale leaps clear of the water ▷

WHALES
AND DOLPHINS

Lionel Bender

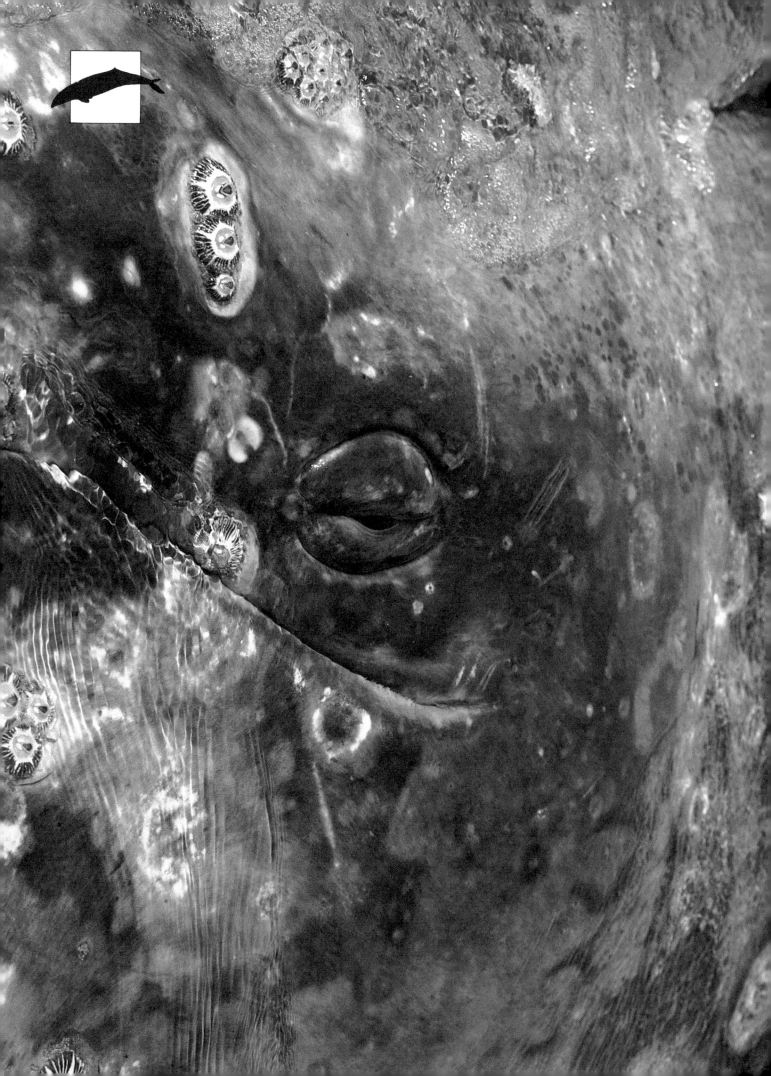

Introduction

The whales include the biggest animals ever known to exist. They also include the fastest swimmers alive. Some, like the Sperm Whale, descend to the ocean depths and are easily the deepest divers among the mammals. The small whales, the dolphins, are some of the most intelligent and playful of animals.

Whales enjoy being in groups and many are friendly towards people. But several kinds of whales have been hunted, by people, almost to extinction.

Because they live completely at sea, little is known about the life of many whales. This book tells just some of the fascinating and surprising things known about these animals. Much more is still to be learned.

The picture opposite shows the head of a Grey Whale

Sea-going mammals

Although whales and dolphins resemble fish, they are in fact mammals like us. They are warm-blooded, they breathe air using lungs, and they give birth to live babies which feed on their mother's milk. Whales had ancestors that lived on land as most mammals do. But for the last 50 million years they have lived in the sea.

Like fish, whales are streamlined for swimming. But a whale swims by up and down movements of its tail, not side to side movements like a fish. Its front limbs are flippers, not fins. These have the same pattern of bones as we have in our arms and hands. The back limbs have disappeared over time. A whale's skin is smooth and has a few hairs while a fish has a scaly skin.

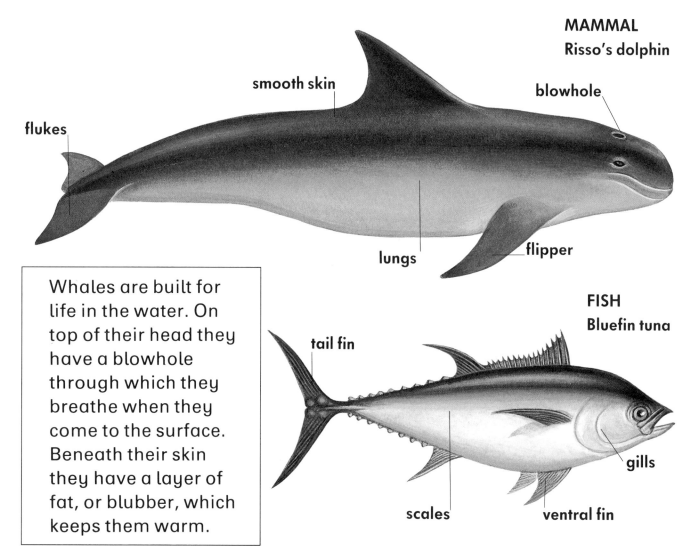

MAMMAL
Risso's dolphin

smooth skin

blowhole

flukes

lungs

flipper

FISH
Bluefin tuna

tail fin

gills

scales

ventral fin

Whales are built for life in the water. On top of their head they have a blowhole through which they breathe when they come to the surface. Beneath their skin they have a layer of fat, or blubber, which keeps them warm.

Although 15 metres long, the Humpback Whale glides easily through the water ▷

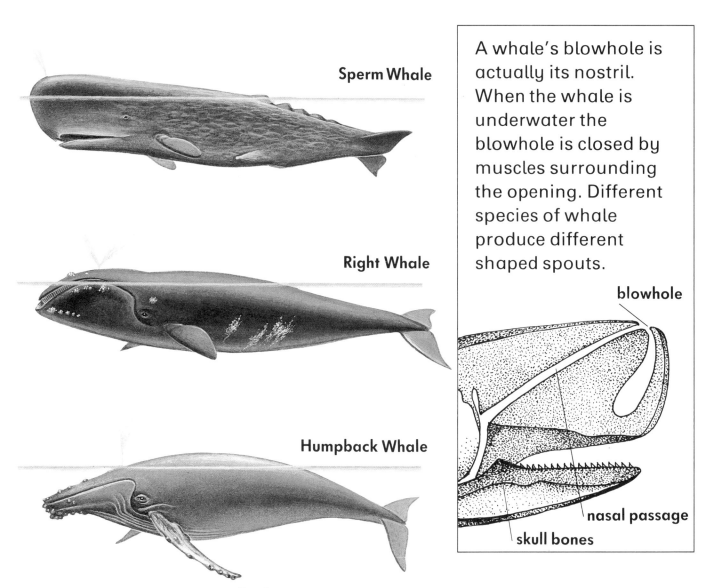

Sperm Whale

Right Whale

Humpback Whale

A whale's blowhole is actually its nostril. When the whale is underwater the blowhole is closed by muscles surrounding the opening. Different species of whale produce different shaped spouts.

blowhole

nasal passage

skull bones

Breathing

Many whales can dive to great depths. A Sperm Whale can go down to more than 3,000 metres and stay underwater for 1½ hours at a time. Yet a whale must come to the surface to breathe. When it resurfaces, it pushes out used air through its blowhole, creating the familiar spout. It then takes a series of deep breaths before diving again.

In proportion to its body size, a whale's lungs are actually smaller than ours. But it fills its lungs much more fully than we do. A whale changes about 90 per cent of the air in its lungs at each breath, while we change only about 12 per cent. It also carries a store of oxygen in its muscles.

◁ **The Blue Whale blows an upright spout up to 10 metres high**

Moving

Even huge species like the 15 metre-long Humpback Whale are natural acrobats and extremely agile swimmers. When they come up from a dive they may launch themselves completely out of the water and twist round in the air before crashing back through the surface. Dolphins often swim in groups in front of ships at sea, riding the bow-waves like surfers.

Whales push themselves through the water by beating their tail flukes up and down with powerful body muscles. They use their flippers for steering. The water rushes easily over their smooth oily skin. They can change the shape of their body surface to cope with the huge water pressure deep in the sea.

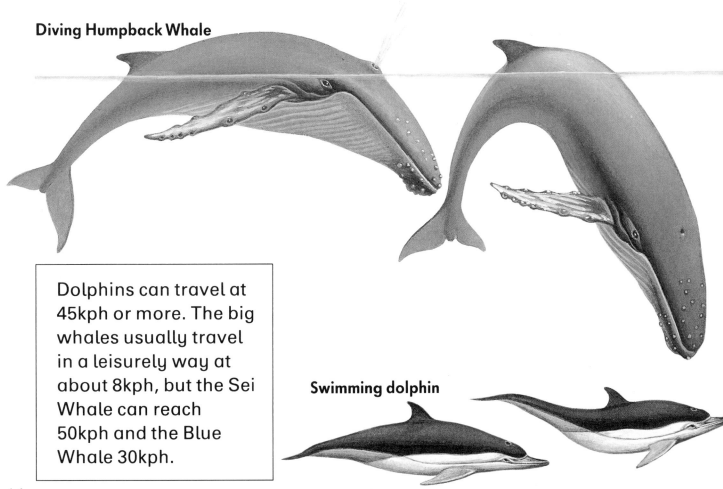

Diving Humpback Whale

Dolphins can travel at 45kph or more. The big whales usually travel in a leisurely way at about 8kph, but the Sei Whale can reach 50kph and the Blue Whale 30kph.

Swimming dolphin

△ **The Blue Whale's tail flukes are seen briefly as it dives**

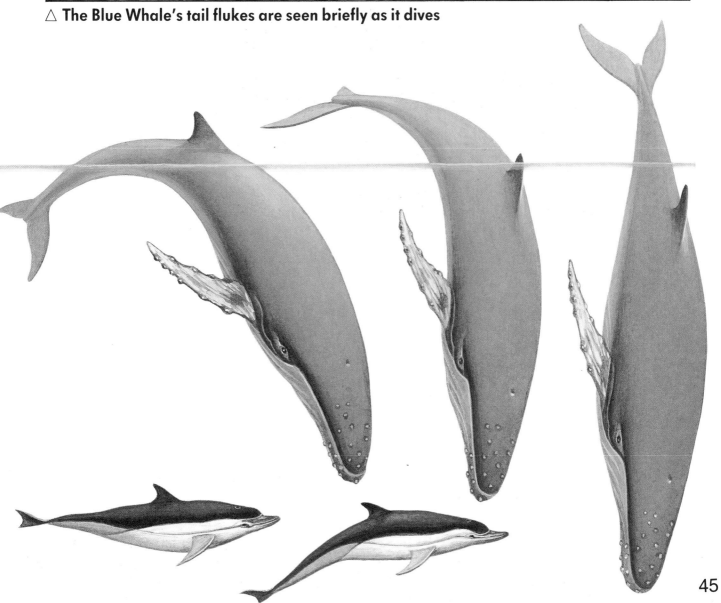

Baleen whales

There are two distinct groups of whales, the baleen and the toothed whales. There are ten species of baleen whales. Instead of teeth they have a series of horny plates with fringed edges hanging from the roof of the mouth. These whalebone plates are called the baleen and are used as a sieve for feeding.

Baleen whales feed on animal plankton – krill and tiny creatures that float in the water. Where these swarm, the whale opens its mouth, takes in sea water, then pushes it out through the fringes. The food items are kept back by the fringes and then swallowed. The Blue Whale, the biggest animal that has ever lived, grows to 150 tonnes on this diet.

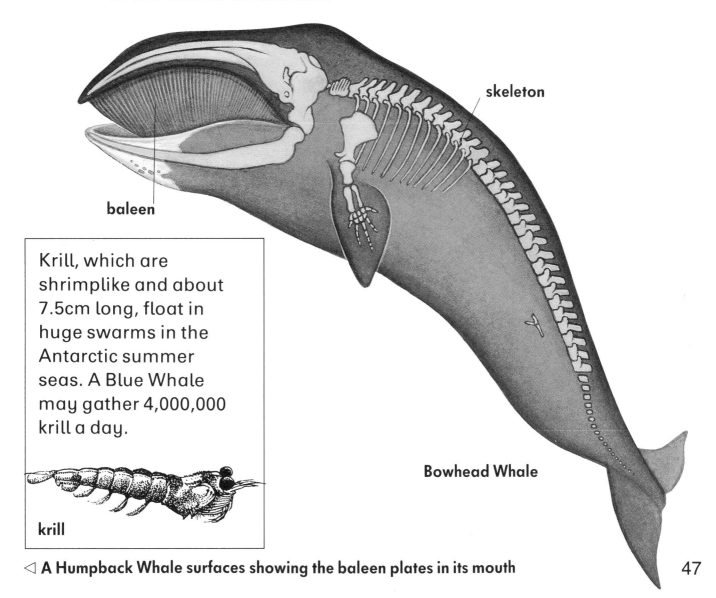

skeleton

baleen

Krill, which are shrimplike and about 7.5cm long, float in huge swarms in the Antarctic summer seas. A Blue Whale may gather 4,000,000 krill a day.

krill

Bowhead Whale

◁ **A Humpback Whale surfaces showing the baleen plates in its mouth**

Toothed whales

Most of the whales in the world, including all the dolphins, are toothed whales. They have jaw bones full of short cone-shaped teeth which they use to hold on to slippery prey like fish and squid. The Common Dolphin has more than 200 teeth. The Sperm Whale, and other species that feed on soft-bodied prey like squid, have less than 50.

The Killer Whale often eats warm-blooded prey such as penguins, seals and even dolphins. It hunts in packs with the whales working together as a team. Some dolphins, like the Bottlenose Dolphin, also feed as a group. They will round up and capture shoals of fish such as tuna.

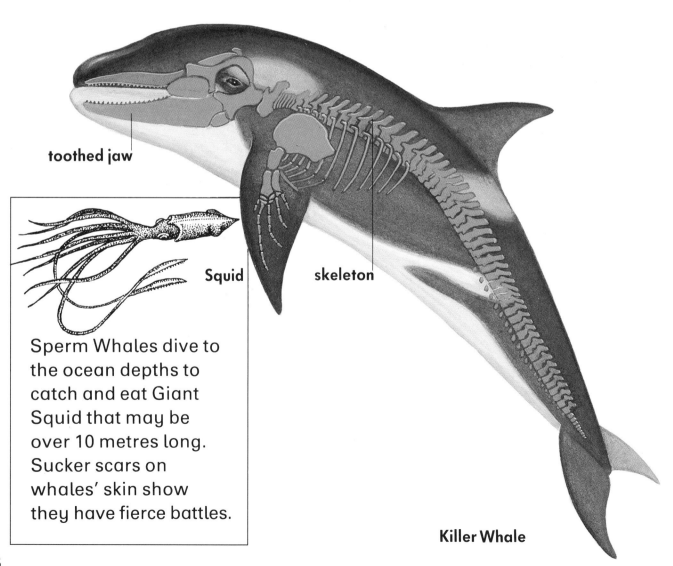

toothed jaw

Squid

skeleton

Sperm Whales dive to the ocean depths to catch and eat Giant Squid that may be over 10 metres long. Sucker scars on whales' skin show they have fierce battles.

Killer Whale

Dolphins and porpoises

The smaller toothed whales include the unicorn-like Narwhal, the White Beluga, the dolphins and the porpoises. Porpoises have a rounded head, without the beak-like jaw which dolphins have. They grow to only about 1.5 metres in length. They have a small top fin or none at all.

Dolphins can grow to about 4 metres long and they have a well-developed top fin. The Bottlenose Dolphin and the Common Dolphin are found almost worldwide, except for polar waters. River dolphins live in large tropical rivers like the Amazon and Indus. They are slow swimmers and sometimes use their long 'beak' to probe the river bed for crabs.

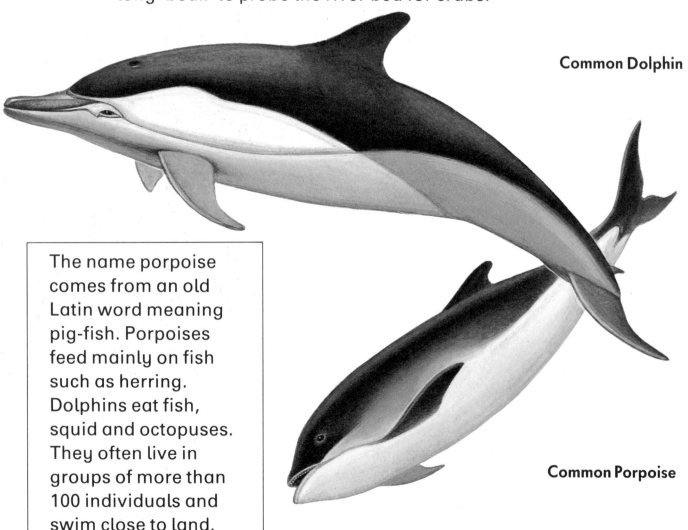

Common Dolphin

Common Porpoise

The name porpoise comes from an old Latin word meaning pig-fish. Porpoises feed mainly on fish such as herring. Dolphins eat fish, squid and octopuses. They often live in groups of more than 100 individuals and swim close to land.

The Bottlenose Dolphin prefers to live in groups ▷

Some whales use echolocation to navigate and find prey. They make high-pitched sounds which are directed forward. Echoes bounce back from prey or the sea floor and are picked up by the whale's ears.

sonar

Shortfin Pilot Whale

Senses and sounds

Like us, whales have a pair of eyes and ears, a nose and a tongue. Whales can see quite well in open air and in shallow water. But because they do not have forward-facing eyes, they cannot judge distances very well. When under water, a whale keeps its nostril closed and so it cannot smell scents. But its tongue can taste chemicals in the water.

Whales do not have large ear openings. But they have excellent hearing and can detect sound waves travelling through the water. Whales make sounds that other whales can hear and respond to. Toothed whales navigate using echolocation, which is similar to the sonar used by ships to navigate.

Beluga Whales ('sea-canaries') have loud and varied voices ▷

Migration

Throughout the year most toothed whales are constantly on the move, following the shoals of fish they feed on. This may take them on endless circuits round the oceans. By contrast, baleen whales make annual to-and-fro journeys between summer feeding and winter breeding areas.

The plankton on which baleen whales feed is most plentiful in Arctic and Antarctic waters during the summer. The Grey Whale migrates 20,000 km from far north to breeding grounds off California. Among Blue Whales, there are Northern and Southern Hemisphere populations. Their breeding grounds lie generally either side of the Equator. The populations do not mix.

Migration route of the Grey Whale

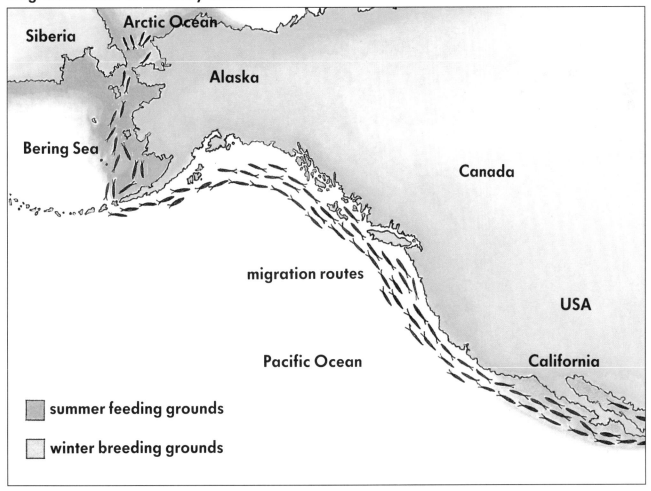

Siberia

Arctic Ocean

Alaska

Bering Sea

Canada

migration routes

USA

Pacific Ocean

California

■ summer feeding grounds

□ winter breeding grounds

◁ **Beluga Whales gather in huge herds as they move south in autumn**

A newborn dolphin has no air in its lungs and it tends to sink. Its mother, or her friends, nudge the baby to the surface where the air stimulates it to open its blowhole and take its first breath. After this it needs no more assistance to breathe or to feed.

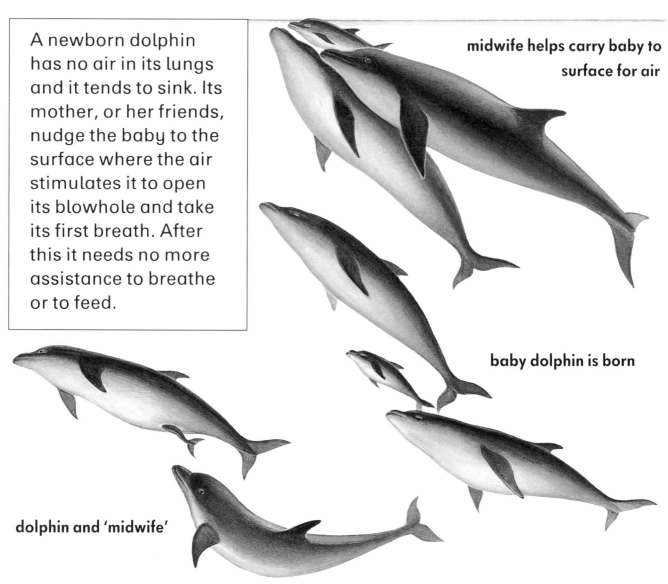

midwife helps carry baby to surface for air

baby dolphin is born

dolphin and 'midwife'

Breeding

Before mating, male toothed whales like the Sperm Whale often fight over females, butting and biting each other for the right to mate. Males of all species usually court the females. They chase them through the water, perform displays of splashing and diving, then swim alongside and stroke and caress them with their head. Even large species like the Humpback Whale have energetic courtship displays, ending with the pair rising out of the water to mate face to face.

In baleen whales, courtship and mating take place in warm tropical waters and the young are born there the following year. In most whales pregnancy lasts for about a year.

A male Grey Whale courts a female under water ▷

Giant babies

Whales have the biggest babies in the world – a Blue Whale calf may be 7.6 metres long and weigh 7,000 kg. They are also some of the fastest growing young, doubling their weight in the first week. The calves take their first feed a few minutes after birth. When the mother suckles the calf, she pumps milk into its mouth which is very thick and rich in fat.

In big baleen whales like the Humpback, Blue and Grey, the mothers produce milk for about six months. By this time the whales have returned to the summer polar feeding grounds where the young can easily find plankton food. The mother can then replace the blubber that she converted to milk.

◁ **A baby Humpback Whale and its mother**

The Blue Whale may weigh as much as 7 tonnes at birth. It grows rapidly at first. Growth slows as it reaches maturity.

1 day (7.5m)

7 months (16m)

5 years old (23m)

25 years old (26m)

By swimming close to its mother a baby whale gets an easier ride ▷

Intelligence

Dolphins appear to be highly intelligent. They have a language of whistles, chirps, clicks and moans that allows them to communicate with one another over great distances. In captivity they learn tricks and are able to copy many sounds and actions made by people. Some scientists believe that they are more intelligent than dogs, but less so than apes.

Some of a whale's intelligent behaviour may just be the result of natural playfulness and friendliness rather than true intelligence. Female whales, for example, automatically help one another to bring up their calves. Dolphins automatically help injured colleagues to the surface to breathe.

An injured Amazon River Dolphin is carried to the surface by three others

Dolphin brains can be bigger than ours. The ratio of brain to body weight gives a rough idea of intelligence. It is 1 to 50 in humans, 1 to 80 in some dolphins.

dolphin brain   **human brain**

◁ **Dolphins can communicate by sounds**

Survival file

For hundreds of years whales have been hunted and killed. Their flesh is still eaten by many people around the world and is also used to make pet foods. Blubber is the source of whale oil that can be used as a fuel. Smokeless candles, lamps and a lubricant oil for machines can also be made from whale products. The whaling industry has been a ruthless destroyer of wildlife. The numbers of many species have dropped dramatically as animals have been killed faster than they can breed. Today whaling is being halted to let populations grow again.

Whales and dolphins are being studied by scientists

The Right Whales were the first to become rare as they were the 'right' (easiest) whales to hunt. Being slow swimmers, they were easily caught by the first sail-boat whaling ships. With the development of engine-powered whaling ships and explosive harpoons all whales became easy targets for the hunters. Then it was the Sperm Whale and the big baleen whales that suffered. In 1931 thirty thousand Blue Whales were killed in the Antarctic. Never again have so many been seen. There are probably little more than ten thousand left in the whole world.

Dolphins are also hunted for meat in some parts of South-east Asia and South America. Many others die trapped in fishing nets.

Conservation measures and falling profits have brought whaling to a standstill in certain countries. But whaling still continues in other parts of the world. For many species numbers have fallen so low that their recovery is now in doubt. Often little is known about how they live. It is only in the last thirty years that dolphins and small whales have been studied in captivity.

The explosive harpoon made it easier to catch and kill big whales

Killer Whales in a marine park

Identification chart

This chart shows about one-fifth of the world's different species of whales and dolphins and indicates where they live. They are drawn to scale. Each section of the grid represents two metres. The Bottlenose Dolphin is the most frequently seen in zoos.

○ North Atlantic
● South Atlantic
● North Pacific
● South Pacific
◐ Indian Ocean
● Rivers

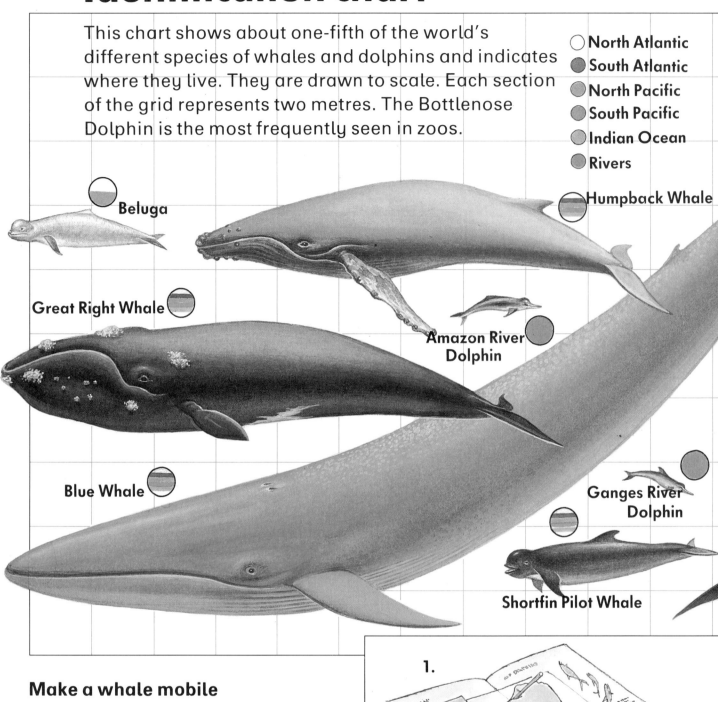

Beluga

Great Right Whale

Humpback Whale

Amazon River Dolphin

Blue Whale

Ganges River Dolphin

Shortfin Pilot Whale

Make a whale mobile

1. Draw or trace whale outlines.
2. Transfer the outlines to a sheet of card.
3. Cut round the edges of each whale.
4. Paint the whales.
5. Make a ring from which to hang the whales.
6. Using cotton thread, attach the whales to the ring and the ring to the ceiling.

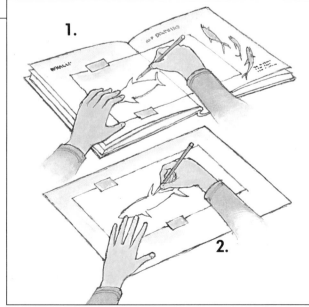

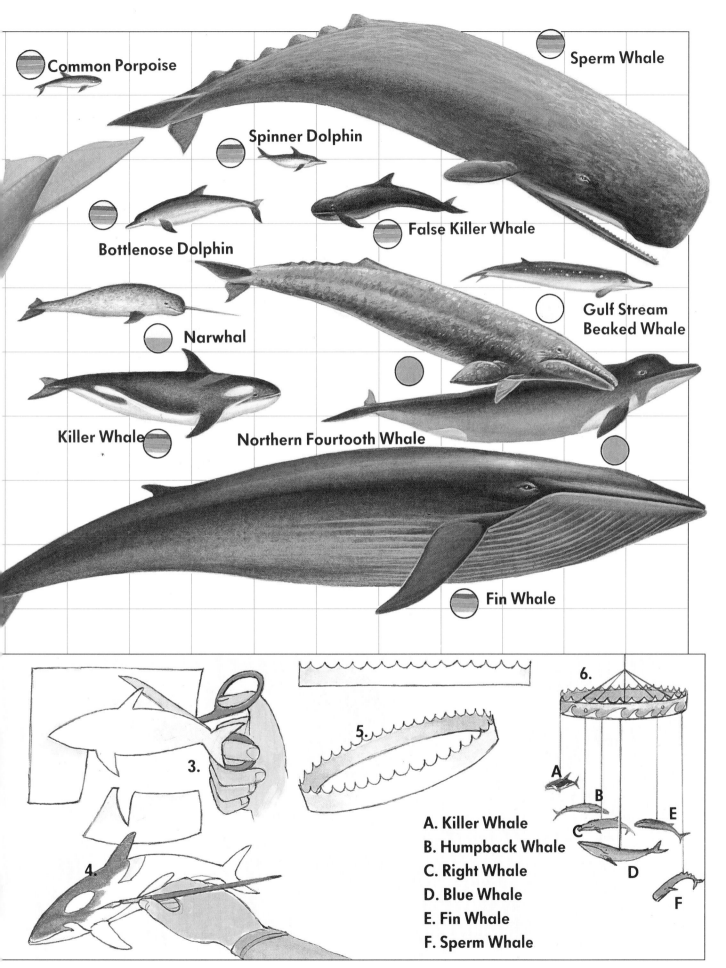

Common Porpoise

Sperm Whale

Spinner Dolphin

False Killer Whale

Bottlenose Dolphin

Gulf Stream
Beaked Whale

Narwhal

Killer Whale

Northern Fourtooth Whale

Fin Whale

3.

4.

5.

6.

A. Killer Whale
B. Humpback Whale
C. Right Whale
D. Blue Whale
E. Fin Whale
F. Sperm Whale

Design
David West
Children's Book Design
Illustrations
Wendie Harris
Tessa Barwick
Picture Research
Cecilia Weston-Baker
Editor
Denny Robson
Consultant
John Stidworthy

This book tells you all about the different types of crocodiles and alligators – where they live, what they eat and how they survive. Find out some surprising facts about them in the boxes on each page. The identification chart at the back of the book will help you when you see crocodiles and alligators in zoos or in the wild.

The little square shows you the size of the animal. Each side represents 2m (6½ft).

A red square means that the animal is in need of protection. See the survival file.

The picture opposite shows a young crocodile hatching from its egg

66

CROCODILES
AND ALLIGATORS
Lionel Bender

Introduction

Crocodiles and alligators are the only survivors of a group of reptiles that dominated the Earth about 200 to 65 million years ago, a group which included the dinosaurs. The crocodile and alligator family consists of 22 species of reptiles that are adapted for life in and around water. The family includes the true crocodiles, which live in Africa, Asia and Australia, the alligators of North and South America and China, the caimans of South America, and the Gharial, or Gavial, of India. Together they are known as crocodilians.

Crocodiles and alligators are most common in hot tropical regions, but they also live in areas where there are warm summers and cool winters. They are all hunters and they feed on animals that range from deer and cattle to fish and birds.

◁ **An American Alligator stretches out of the water to catch a young Egret**

◁ **A crocodile basks in the sun on a riverbank**

midday

Most crocodiles keep their bodies at 30-35°C (85-97°F). This is a few degrees cooler than ours. They become sluggish at below 20°C (68°F).

morning

evening

When the sun gets too hot, the crocodile slinks into the water.

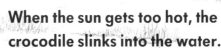

A crocodile warms up by basking in the morning sun.

It warms up again in late afternoon and early evening.

Cold-blooded

Crocodiles and alligators, like other reptiles, are cold-blooded. This means they cannot adjust their body temperature by producing body heat, as we can. They have to rely on their surroundings to keep their bodies warm enough to work properly. This is why they are most common in warm countries.

When they are active, or as they bask in the sun, their temperature rises. Crocodiles and alligators usually lie with their mouths open when they are too hot. This helps them lose heat. They cannot sweat to cool down. But when their temperature increases well above normal, they must stop moving, rest in the shade, or slink into the water.

Life in water

Crocodilians are difficult to see when they lie in the water. They are often mistaken for logs. Their eyes and nostrils are set high on their heads. This means that they can see and breathe when they are floating almost totally underwater. They use sideways sweeps of their large, powerful, flattened tails to swim along. When danger threatens, they sink quickly downwards and backwards using a sudden upward movement of their webbed hind feet.

Underwater, crocodilians keep their nostrils and ears closed. A special flap of skin sweeps sideways across each eye to give protection during diving. The animals can hold their breath for more than an hour.

A Gharial swimming in a river, showing the sideways motion of its tail

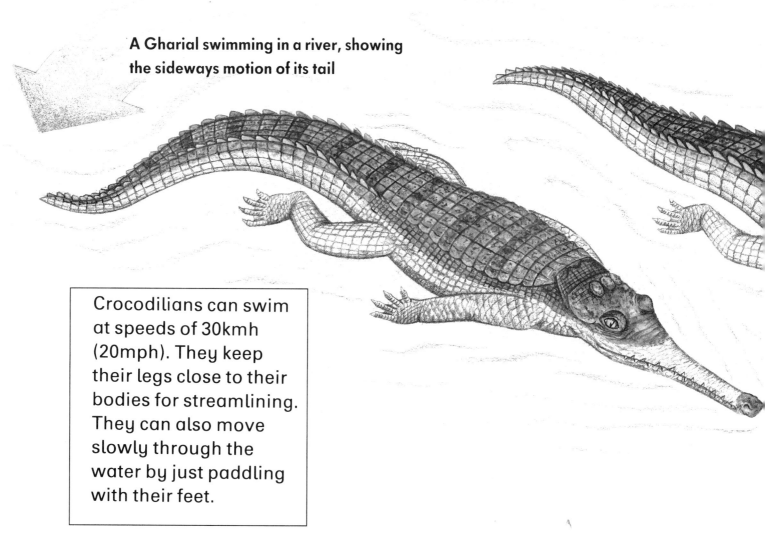

Crocodilians can swim at speeds of 30kmh (20mph). They keep their legs close to their bodies for streamlining. They can also move slowly through the water by just paddling with their feet.

An American Alligator cruises through the water

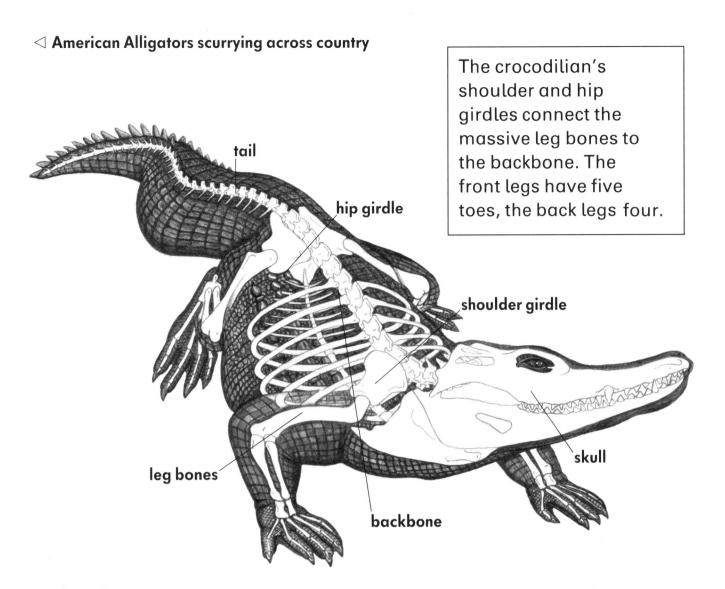

tail

hip girdle

The crocodilian's shoulder and hip girdles connect the massive leg bones to the backbone. The front legs have five toes, the back legs four.

shoulder girdle

skull

leg bones

backbone

Out on land

The Australian Freshwater Crocodile and the Nile Crocodile can gallop across country, with front and back legs working together like a bounding squirrel. But usually crocodiles walk on dry land by stretching their legs and lifting their bodies well off the ground. Alligators and caimans usually slink about, moving slowly forward on their stomachs with their legs spread out either side.

The Gharial and the Saltwater Crocodile of South-east Asia rarely move more than a few metres from their river and estuary homes. But species that live in ponds and lakes, such as the Indian Marsh Crocodile, may travel many kilometres overland in search of water if their homes dry up.

Big and small

Crocodiles and alligators grow rapidly in areas where they can find plenty of food and it is warm all year round. The biggest crocodilian on record was an Estuarine Crocodile from Bengal that is thought to have measured 10m (33ft) in length and weighed more than two tonnes. The Smooth-fronted Caiman and African Dwarf Crocodile, on the other hand, barely reach 1.5m (5ft) as adults.

Crocodilians continue to grow throughout their lives and they can live for many years – American Alligators may live for up to 70 years. This means that several species can grow very large. But today poachers kill the largest specimens and so individuals over 6m (20ft) long are rare.

A Dwarf Caiman looks for a meal with only its head out of the water

The Estuarine Crocodile, like all crocodilians, continues to grow throughout its life ▷

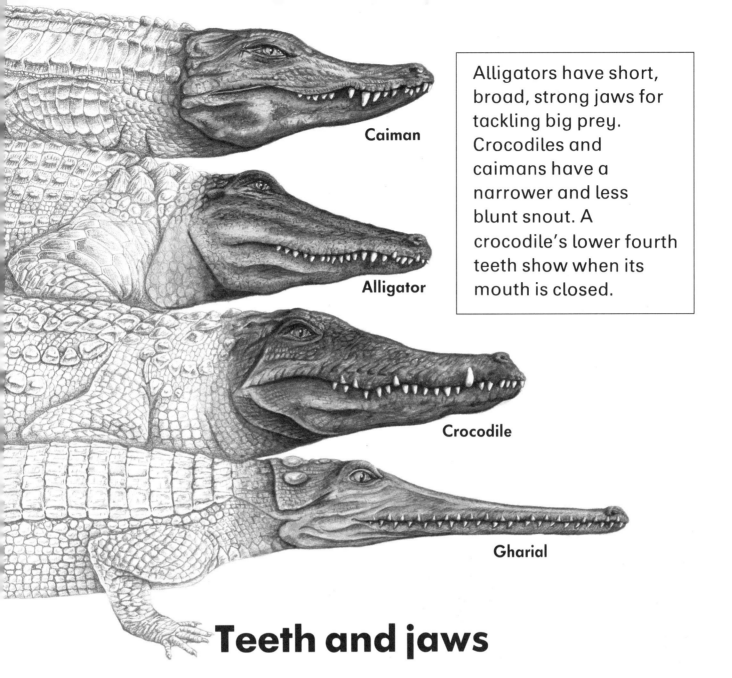

Caiman

Alligator

Alligators have short, broad, strong jaws for tackling big prey. Crocodiles and caimans have a narrower and less blunt snout. A crocodile's lower fourth teeth show when its mouth is closed.

Crocodile

Gharial

Teeth and jaws

The Gharial is a fish-eater which has about 160 teeth. These are small and pointed so that the animal can keep hold of its slippery prey. Crocodiles and alligators have about 100 teeth. Their teeth are good for holding flesh, but not for cutting or chewing it. Crocodiles hold food in their teeth and thrash it about to tear it apart. They can then swallow the food in large chunks.

Crocodiles and alligators often lose teeth in struggles with large prey. But the teeth are quickly replaced. Each tooth contains a small replacement tooth inside it. A crocodilian may produce fifty or more sets of teeth within its lifetime.

◁ **A Gharial with its bulb-like nose**

Hunting and feeding

Fish, birds, snakes, lizards, frogs, turtles, rats, deer, zebra and cattle are all part of the diet of crocodiles, alligators and caimans. As babies, however, crocodilians eat mainly insects, frogs and small fish. The Gharial eats nothing but fish.

The American Alligator often captures prey by lying in wait in shallow water or within pools along the river bank. As a victim approaches, the alligator seizes it, drags it underwater and then tears it apart. Crocodiles sometimes attack and eat one another. They will even eat people. But this only happens when they cannot find their normal prey. Crocodilians also feed on dead animals – they are both scavengers and hunters.

A young crocodile grips a fish in its pointed teeth

A Nile Crocodile eats a zebra killed by another hunter ▷

Attack and defence

A crocodilian's most effective weapons are its powerful jaws. Once these are closed tight, no animal can escape their grip. A crocodilian will sometimes use its tail to knock over an animal before trying to eat it. Male alligators fight over females at mating time, tearing at each other with their teeth.

Despite their fierceness, crocodiles and alligators do have enemies. Crocodiles may be killed in fights with lions and leopards. A mother elephant or hippo will also attack a crocodile that threatens her young. But most crocodilians are so well camouflaged in drab greens and browns that they usually surprise and then easily overpower their prey.

Male alligators will often attack one another fiercely

An American Alligator, covered with and surrounded by algae, waits for a meal ▷

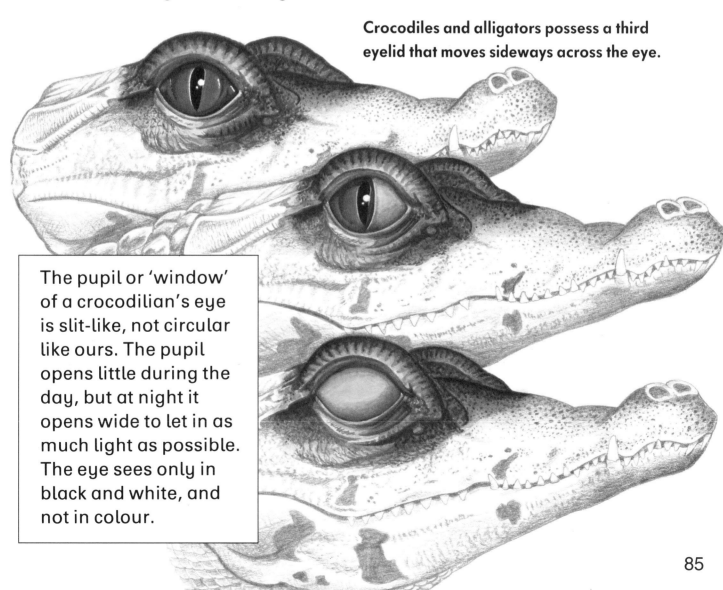

⊲ **A crocodile roars to attract a mate**

Senses and sounds

Vision and hearing are crocodilians' most important senses. They rely mainly on vision to hunt and capture prey. When their ears are out of the water, they can hear well too. They keep in touch with one another using a variety of sounds. Baby crocodiles peep loudly when they hatch from their eggs so that their mother will help them out of the nest. Male and female crocodilians roar and croak loudly at each other at mating time.

Crocodiles and alligators swallow their food underwater in large chunks and so they do not need good senses of smell and taste. Their skin is thick and leathery and not very sensitive to touch.

Crocodiles and alligators possess a third eyelid that moves sideways across the eye.

The pupil or 'window' of a crocodilian's eye is slit-like, not circular like ours. The pupil opens little during the day, but at night it opens wide to let in as much light as possible. The eye sees only in black and white, and not in colour.

Courtship and mating

At mating time, the male crocodilian courts the female. An adult male Gharial has a swelling on its snout that probably helps to attract a mate. A male Nile Crocodile displays his desire to mate by thrashing about in the water and keeping his mouth open. He comes alongside the female in the water and puts his legs on her back. The pair then sink to the bottom of the river or lake and mate.

About two months after mating, the female is ready to lay her eggs. While she is pregnant she prepares a nest, which acts as an incubator to protect the eggs and keep them warm. The male rarely helps in nest building, or in looking after the eggs.

A male Gharial (left) approaches a female as a plover looks on

A female Estuarine Crocodile guards her nest ▷

An alligator's egg showing the developing embryo within the fluid-filled sac

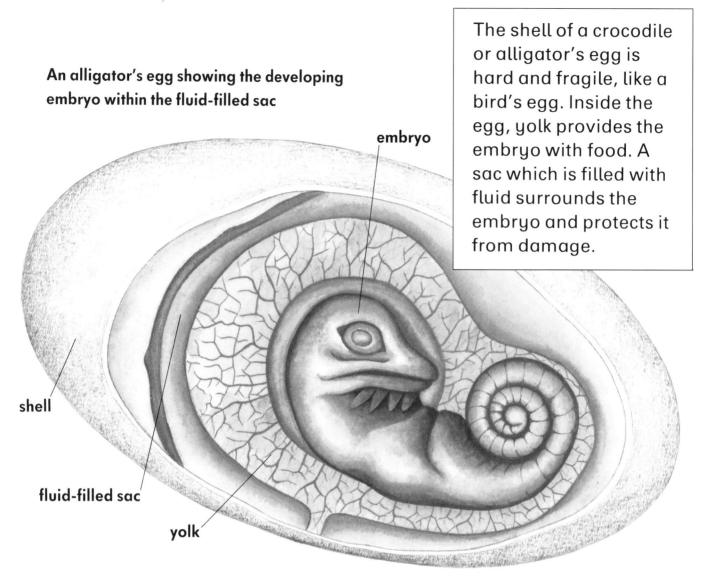

embryo

shell

fluid-filled sac

yolk

The shell of a crocodile or alligator's egg is hard and fragile, like a bird's egg. Inside the egg, yolk provides the embryo with food. A sac which is filled with fluid surrounds the embryo and protects it from damage.

Eggs and hatchlings

A female alligator or female Gharial lays between 15 and 80 eggs. A female Nile Crocodile lays as many as 90, each the size of a goose egg. The Gharial digs out a hollow in the ground for a nest. Alligators make a heap of water plants, lay the eggs on the top, then cover them with more plant material. Crocodiles often just bury their eggs in the sand.

The baby crocodilians hatch between nine and 17 weeks later. Sometimes the mother picks up eggs that have not hatched and gently crushes them in her jaws to free the young. Hatchlings look like small versions of their parents. Even those of the 6m (20ft) long Nile Crocodile are less than 30cm (12in) in length.

Young crocodilians often hatch within moments of each other ▷

Growing up

Newborn crocodiles and alligators cannot look after themselves very well. Many are eaten by fish, birds, mammals and other reptiles, especially large lizards such as monitors. However, their mothers usually protect them for the first few months. Nile and Estuarine Crocodile mothers often carry their young from the nest to the water in their mouths. A mother Gharial will carry her young on her back.

The young grow quickly, almost doubling their length in the first year. The American Alligator grows 25 to 30cm (10 to 12in) each year. It is adult when it is five years old. Most crocodilians are ready to mate by the time they are eight years old.

A young alligator hitches a ride on its mother's back

A young crocodile about to devour a crab ▷

Survival file

In many parts of Africa, South America, Australia and India, the native people kill alligators and crocodiles for food. This hunting has been going on for hundreds of years. But because these people only kill as many animals as they need, they do not threaten the survival of crocodilians. Since the 1950s, however, commercial hunters have killed crocodilians in their tens of thousands just for their skins. The skins are used to make handbags, shoes and wallets which are sold in shops all over the world.

In a nature reserve, crocodiles are given water buffalo to eat

Crocodiles and alligators are now also threatened by local farmers, who destroy their homes. The farmers drain lakes, ponds and swamps for land on which to graze their animals or grow crops. In India, hunting and habitat destruction reduced the number of Gharials in the wild to less than 100 in 1974.

Since about 1975, there has been a worldwide ban on trade in the skins of most crocodiles and alligators. But illegal hunting and egg-collecting still go on. There is also a growing trade in capturing crocodilians to be shown in wildlife parks and kept as pets. Most of those sold as pets are killed once they get too big.

Trade in crocodilian skins continues

Rangers sometimes have to kill alligators

In India, Australia and America, there are now crocodile and alligator farms that are helping to increase the numbers of crocodilians in the wild. Eggs are taken from the wild and kept safely in incubators. The hatchlings are looked after and fed until they are big and strong enough to be released back into the wild. The young are taken to rivers and lakes around the world.

Identification chart

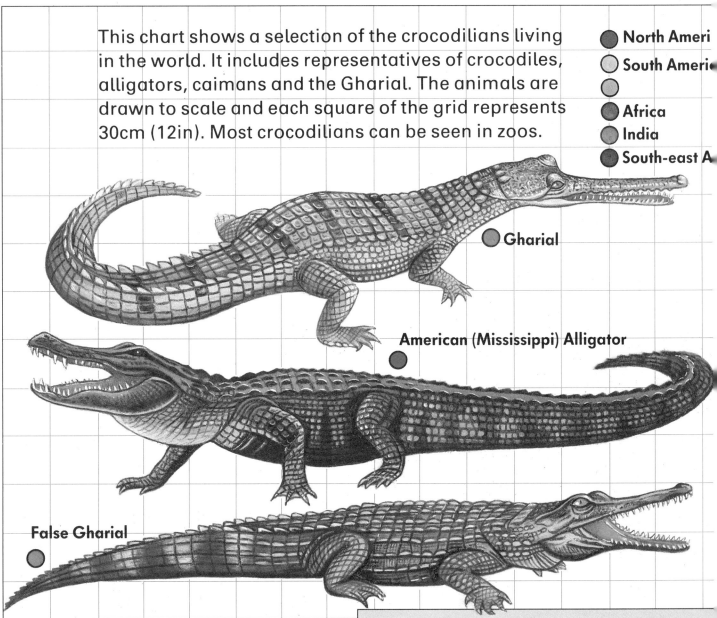

This chart shows a selection of the crocodilians living in the world. It includes representatives of crocodiles, alligators, caimans and the Gharial. The animals are drawn to scale and each square of the grid represents 30cm (12in). Most crocodilians can be seen in zoos.

- ● North Ameri
- ○ South Ameri
- ●
- ● Africa
- ● India
- ● South-east A

● Gharial

American (Mississippi) Alligator ●

False Gharial ●

Make Crocodilian Snap

1. Trace the heads of the four types of crocodilian shown on these pages onto pieces of cardboard.

2. Make about six of each type of playing card.

3. Use the cards to play Snap or Pairs, matching the shapes of the heads and tooth patterns.

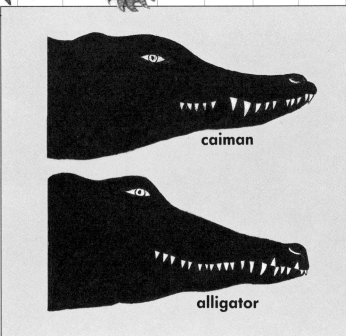

caiman

alligator

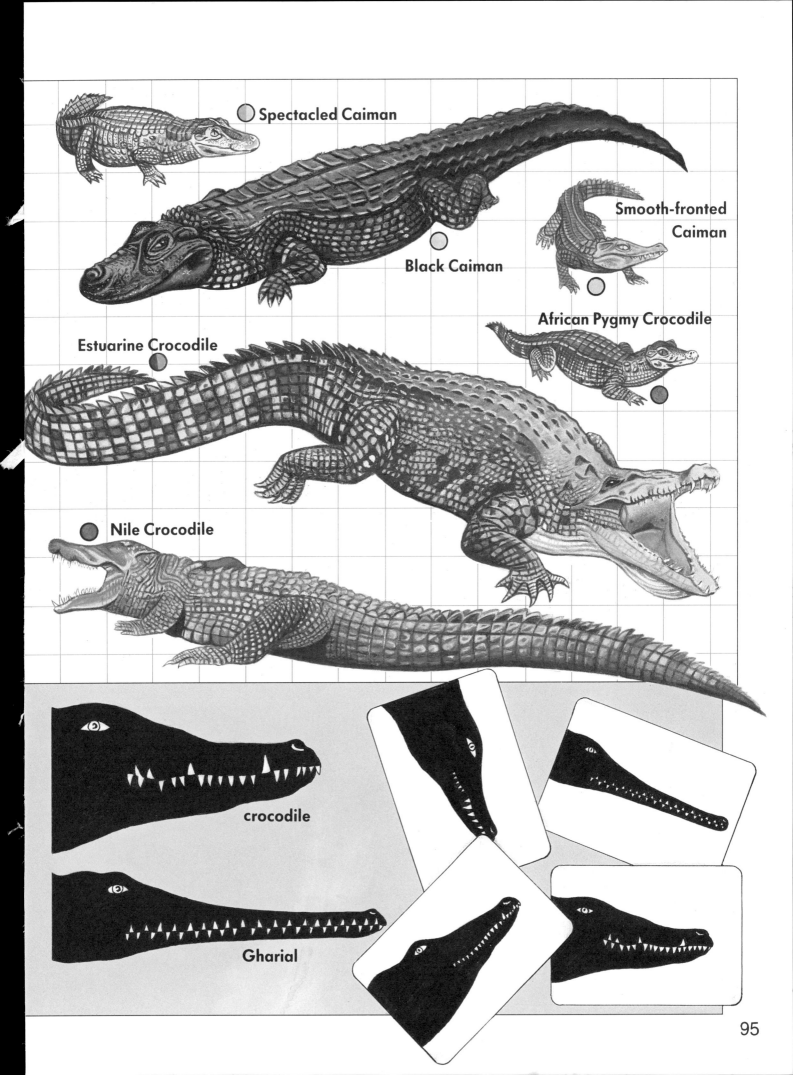

Spectacled Caiman

Black Caiman

Smooth-fronted Caiman

African Pygmy Crocodile

Estuarine Crocodile

Nile Crocodile

crocodile

Gharial

ACKNOWLEDGEMENTS

Photographic credits

Ardea: 10, 18, 25, 26, 35 (bottom), 39, 45, 51, 53, 74, 78, 86, 90;
Bruce Coleman: 27, 42, 49, 62, 63, 67, 68, 70, 73, 76, 77, 82, 83, 87, 89, 93 (top);
Frank Lane Picture Agency: 17, 80, 91; Planet Earth: 7, 9, 13, 20, 22, 23, 29, 34,
35 (top), 41, 46, 57, 58, 60, 63, 81, 84, 92; Frank Spooner Agency: 93 (bottom);
Survival Anglia: 54, 59, 62 (inset); Zefa: 14, 30, 37.